I Have a Pipe

I Have a Pipe

Poems and Pictures by

Joseph S. Sturgeon

ISBN-13: 978-0615903941 (code1635 press)
ISBN-10: 0615903940

www.code1635.net

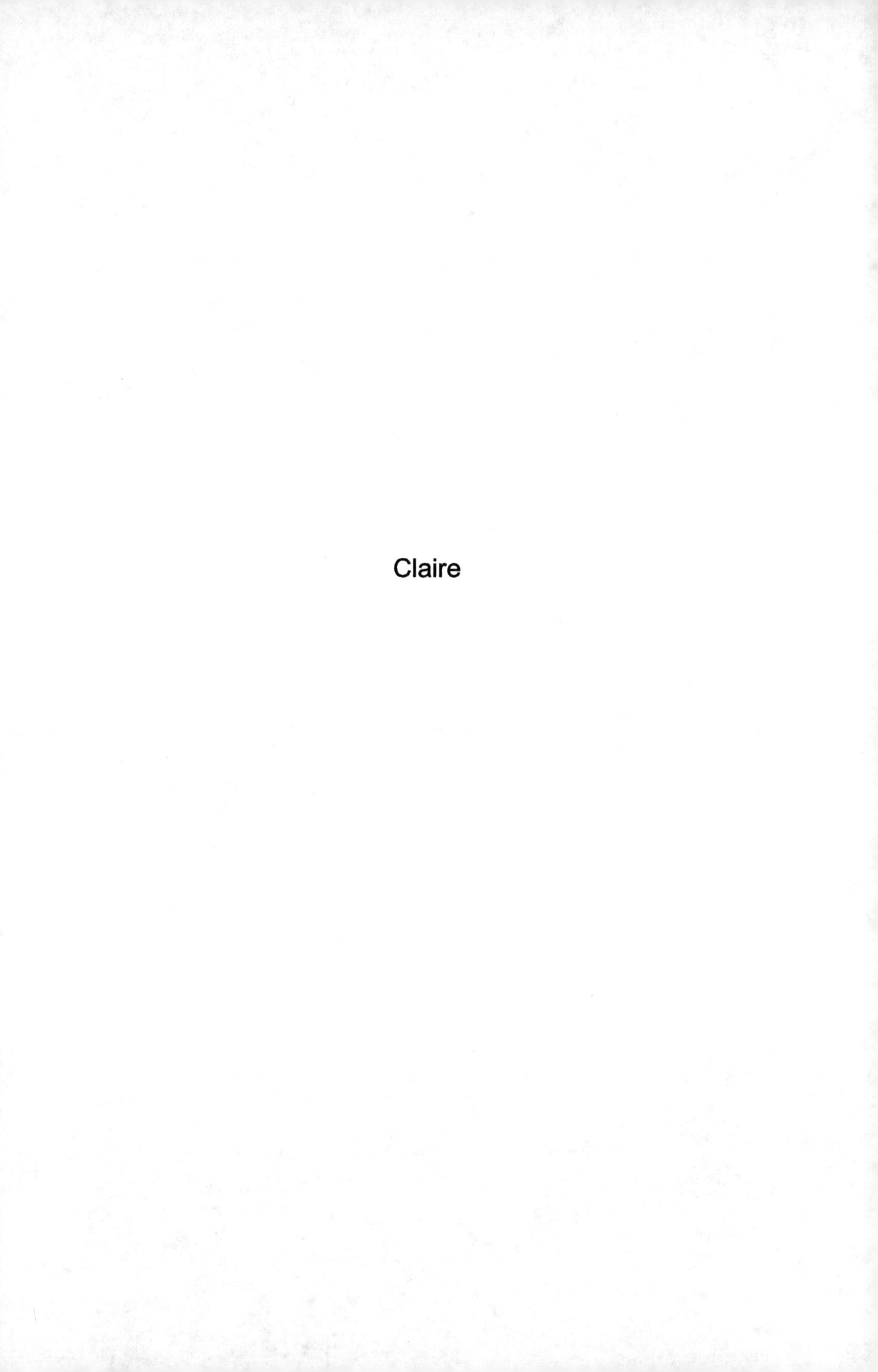

Claire

Contents

I have a pipe loaded with obsession.
Smoke, the ghost of fire,
Flies at me furiously.
What can you love that is not loved?

If by touch I could lay a sweetness
Through your body that would spread
Like dawn across the horizons
Of all that you will see and feel,

If with a magic word I could unchain
That breathless tune from your lips
And have the universe sigh and release
All the locks and seals and vows on souls,

If through a ray from my eye I could guide
Your ship as it searched the wine dark sea
To a turquoise bay where waves would lap
For pulsing hours the endless sands of desire,

That then would be enough me,
But for you, would never be.

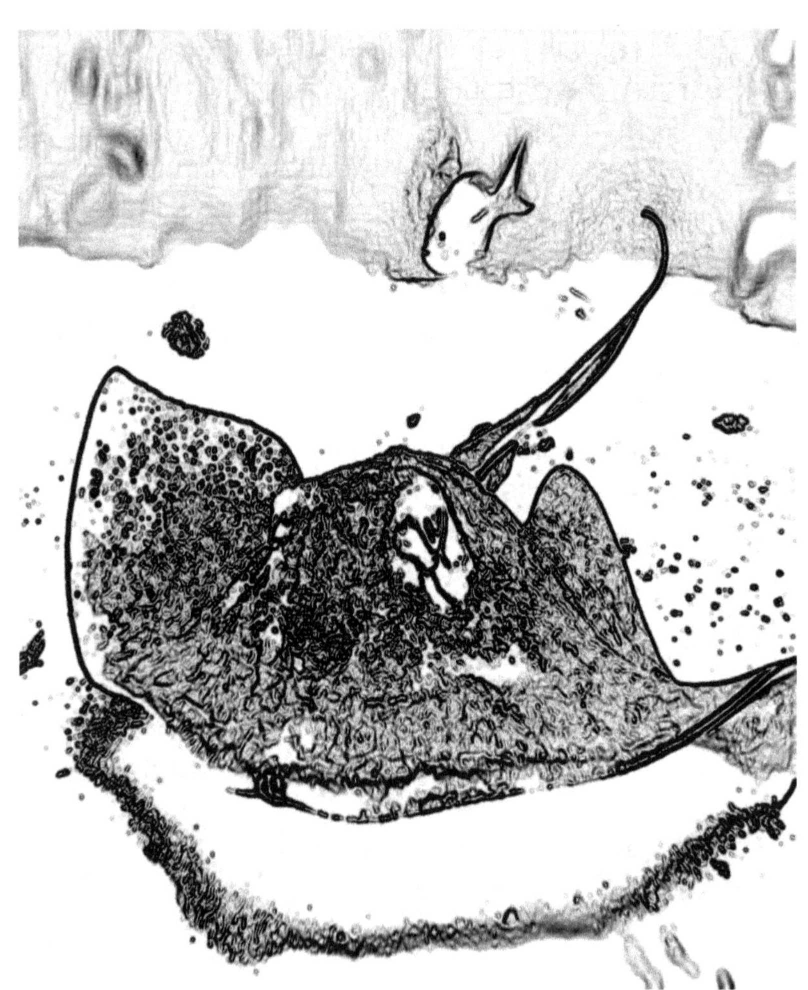

Stingrays will strike at your heart
When you, shortsighted, glide fearlessly
Over them and muscle in too close.
Do not remove the barb!
Carry it and the ray to the clinic.

It's your baby now and you must learn
To nurse your new responsibility
And care for its safety. For if it dies
Because you overdosed on speed,
The withdrawal will begin a warming.

Your last sensation will melt the icecaps,
Sink the final twisted movement
Of the sucking whirlpool that pulls
The mortal touch toward the chilled deep,
That seemed to crush salvation that day.

The final twitch is stillness, nothing cold.
The quivering dews are blankets unused
By days secured and sleep protected.

A well known person of our age,
Has said, I read,
That good is not harmonious,
But numerous and at times conflicting.

Maybe he is a man of many gods
Or a pantheist looking under stones,
Or an infidel raising idols,
Or an astrologer invoking stars.

No, he is not.
He is reasonable, polished and enlightened.
But good or goods, one or many,
Is still a bewildering forest.

Another man, running away from language
To language,
Could not go on, but must go on.
Is this that good or good enough?

Cast out the relativists.
Cover them with dung.
Gather up the absolutists.
Let them all be hung.

Abstractions seldom break and readily reproduce,
As is known by the pixies who studied silver salts
Or zoomed the screen and found the final color boxed.

Known too by the string people who would chew
Long hours on progression's rib, symmetry's other claw,
To avoid the cream pie tossed in chocolate gossip.

That they are and That is something Jamesian:
The moral striptease first arose among the Gypsies,
Who augured under pyramids and eyed your dime.

But cardinal enumerations for most will do the job,
And from a kitchen strainer working well with time
The perfect grain for daily bread a cone will find.

Dark matters, dark energies and old historic ethers
Are still obliged to their projections on the screen
Of hard rock wall that stumbles, crumbles and falls.

单词

All, nothing or this embalmed, gray thing,
The Word,
In between and misbegotten.
Seven white irises,
Above the yellow flag

TOYOTA
Bud

As we will be players and not forgive
The line and meter haphazardly stained
When inklings burnished memory, we live
Repeats, guffaws and sorrows tamed.

No harm to take reflection's peaceful place.
Our farm a niche will nurture lighter beasts
Than heroes trampling history to trace
Epics, tooth and claw, of clans deceased.

For soon the vaulted, enterprising dome
Lowered, will not house such levered thought
That shapes horizons far and close to home,
Dispersion houses souls our plague has wrought.

No more the leading act of ventures grand
We watch the gleaming deathless from the stands.

As light as wraiths the rollers congregate
Below the shining street light. Moths
With skinny legs in cotton shorts await
The rite of rolling-down to darkness softened.

That day another wheel had met the hill.
Taming blades trimmed the hope of weeds
To seed the summer breeze with thyme and dill,
To sacrifice the rhyme, to still the deeds.

Their arms all tucked like logs the cautious roll
Side wise, descending screaming joy.
The acrobatic brave tumble, flip, console,
The timid with cocky grins of fear avoided.

As we role along the rough is planed.
The sin, the fall, atoned by greener stain.

Erichthonius

As the sky
    Had no boundaries,
    Breathlessly he could ascend,
For his balls
    Are inflated balloons
    Her seduction enlarged,
With her prayer
    She ensnared
    The armory vaults.

Revelations of zeal,
    Off the wings,
    That Zenith discharged,
Was a rain,
    A refrain
    From the artisan forge,
That warm drops
    From the heights
    Congeal in the soil.

Beneath the water,
        lily launching pads
Larva measure
        worth in parted lips.
Rhetorical circumference
        in ponds
Persuades the birthing
        more than wider hips.

In amniotic fluid
        time is keeping
Children in denser realms
        to please the sun.
The periods of sacrifice
        find deeper
Beats, and the voice of nymphs
        is slowly sung.

Bullfrogs devour protein,
        their hoard off spring,
And sibling spirits
        imagine a fate,
Diaphanous, when a fluttered
        stress on wing
Will alternate
        the time with blood and mates.

Would those who chew their words to spit
        them out,
Let amphibious meter tender doubt?

Sorry

Click, click, yes there is a cult, sorry Charlie.
But wait, hey wait just a minute, is there a diploma,
A book, a movie, a dissertation, a mere entry
In the can. And here he was dressed to kill
Ready to set hook and get his morsel:
E pluribus unions, hoi polloi, hoidy-toidy
The high roof of the gleaming sea our bait.

Now watch out! Here come the shepherds
And the set up waiting with the crook,
But what a part and check out the line
Of bewildering mono-filament, ten pound test.
Resentment, doubled and redoubled smooth,
In a viscous media. It buoys the aspirations
Of whiskered bottom feeders. Clam up!

The Word rewound too tight by spinners gray,
Employing scholars bloated, students gaunt,
To rectify historic guides, will fade.
Lockjaw inflames the scratch that haunts.

Can this, a take on saying no, to points
That keep a species gorged beyond itself,
Reflect in ponds the fallen notes conjoined
As stones from heavens feed the mirror's wealth?

We fucked Nebraska, Kansas too, we drifted in
And out and left behind a section residue
Of bible thumpers bearing hoes as sins
Imposed by money lender banking dudes.

A faith in souls, or selves, is laced with lust,
Abandon bleeding Kansas redressed in dust.

Did we not know that the thing could be read darkly?
Each zealous convert now aiming at the ridiculous,
Grinning face beneath the masking tears and smile,
So sure that the first readings were so final, so firm,
Could not suspect the arrogance of that first step.

The pudgy legs were quivering, but the ground,
Was solid, supported by ancient trunks and columns.

The reeds dissolve the shallow light at noon,
Minor chords on moaning cellos swell,
Beneath the cane that shades an August moon,
Shadow songs reweave her bamboo shell.

A boat, the bow embracing varnished wings,
Of rippling waves moonlit and pale,
A roiling crescendo, taunting strings,
Was the husky flight of fluttering veils.

When choirs no longer sing about the sea,
And violins don't echo her arching voice,
She'll sail away from dancing reeds and he,
Shroud of allegros, can forget her choice.

Fierce tempo sends desire a silent note,
A tear to fill the score unborn -- we float.

krackel
HERSHEY'S
krackel
MILK CHOCOLATE AND CRISPED RICE
HERSHEY'S
MILK CHOCOLATE
HERSHEY'S
MILK CHOCOLATE

The bags of chocolate mini bars remain
Behind a while to treat a multi-pack
Of sweet to bitter-sweet diminished ghosts.
The wrappers too are stirred by hidden hands
That dive beneath the silver waves to find
The mound of monsters smoothly melts away.

Gulf of Tonkin Resolutions

Our Enemy now comes full frontal.
Diversions, previously deployed, are seen through
As shaft the heroes are all dead. Their brains
And magic potions spilt on the slippery floor.
Escape tunnels have collapsed and the plans
For final victory are burning, illegible, smoking,
Indifferently in cabinets plundered or unopened.
Some are bargaining still and offering
Their rotting limbs and sickened children
While in corners and backed to the wall
The formerly strong are frozen, plaster figures,
Without reason cocking unloaded weapons.
Still now lonely this bunker
And the shinning eye of passing time with the dying.

Have we by parsing seconds, shredding space,
Rewrote the code or keenly carved more blunt
Necessities? For organs bound by race
Will have their bloody path aligned to hunt.

Yet still, we heard the slayer stop to pray,
Echoing all, his bray returned a psalm.
Nothing sings that holds a note from swaying
Time, time to die or read a palm.

Her breathing, rising turns the quiver out
To scream delivery. The arrow points
Exhaustingly, a higher grounding shouts
The marching song of boastful boys anointed.

We linger here among the broken bones
Of God, to chirp preludes that might atone.

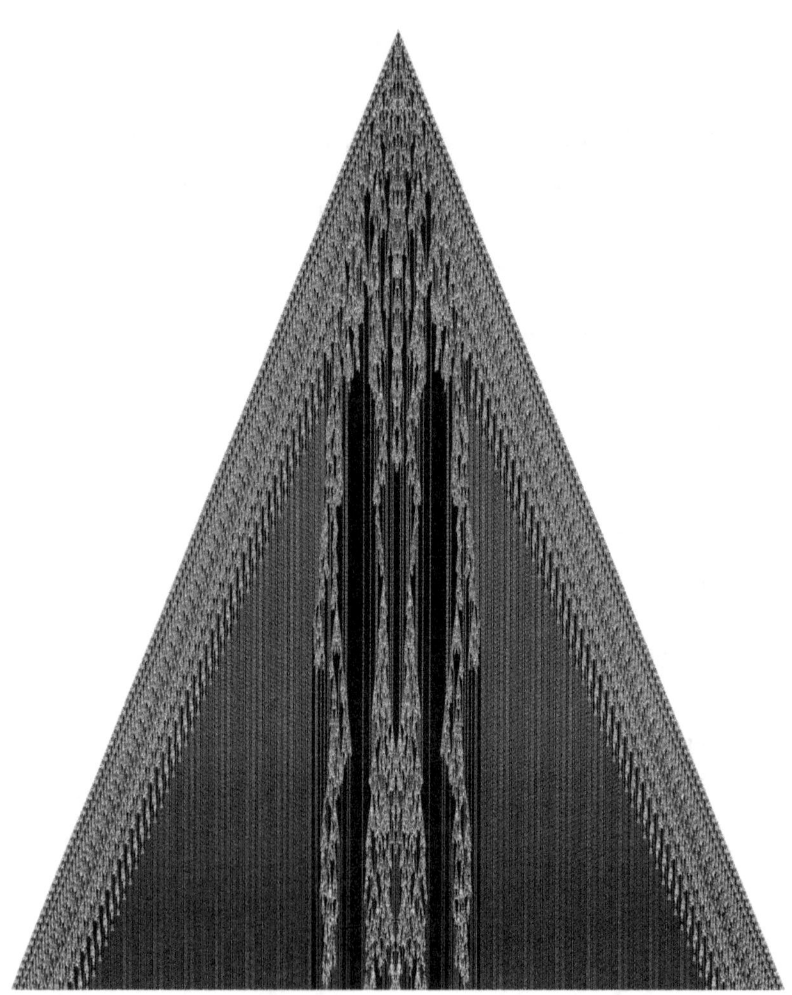

No calling brings the sun to earth today.
Warming trends, the hope of weathermen
Have bombed Hanoi with acid gray.
Stirring love, the finger points back then.

Of those that hold unfolding nature's spread
Includes the bloodless tooth that craves insight:
As meat is held between the legs of bread,
The baguette tastes of long departed bites.

The alchemy of lasting rites will spare
The rutting call of father's maul to nail
The last of men to crosses well repaired
And let evolving pattern flow unjailed.

The prison house we made of thought is home.
We need but little room on earth to roam.

matica alla testa dei popoli socia-
listi, la garanzia migliore della
pace nel mondo e della collabo-
razione operosa fra le nazioni.

Sette Federico

Bisceglie 19-12-1949

All'Associazione
Italia U.R.S.S.
Via XX Settembre, 3
Roma

The poet dictator has a mustache but no beard
To blur the jut and dimple of rhyme and reason.
The razor trims his prophecies each day close
To the barked insistence of his five year plan.

For servants the pile around the barber's chair
Will make a course felt hat, stuff a winter overcoat,
A home for whiskered muttering of the chill
That casts the statue of their coming glory.

But this, though closer is no more true to things
Then any other creation myth claiming makers,
Potters and fornicating fabricators
Who would not pluck the facile wisdom free.

That what fruits abundantly through time,
Like being is, is not the dread of scarcities refined
Through preciousness. The clawing grasp that carves
It's name on newborn skin will never touch.

7
20
PAPUA NEW GUINEA
PAPUA NEW GUINEA
PAPUA NEW GUINEA
PAPUA NEW GUINEA

Old Dad is pumping mother loads. Get back,
Form ranks with tribal elders pendant fangs.
The shack infants are bawling blame for lack
Of murder's milk revenging fathers gang.

Conforming love to stalk the nearest face,
Totemic genes imprint the talk of grander
Armies spread across the common race,
While atoms pressing inward still meander.

The death clause though musty still provokes
A mutinous urge on madness ripe with age,
A swagger prance for boys who see no joke
In flickered frames where hallowed legends rage.

Entombed alive in nervous cells they scream
To blow apart the reason they would redeem.

Modifiers remove one by one the nails and bolts
That piously attach the bully pulpit to its plinth.
Where, teetering to the chuckles of the congregated,
It must play the straight man to the pratfall end.

And though the levitated audience will always retreat
Back below the elevation of their disdain,
The carnival still holds reversal up to nature
Who can see the imitation and still not hear the joke.

Democratic man admires a shifty character
In the hero's part but still keeps the role in play
To forever underestimate assertions of the inner
Bumpkin and return on a dime the levered threat.

The two masks, justified only in each other eyes,
By some future archeology will be uncovered
And, displayed in the holographic Museum of Deep
Consciousness, seem less grim than wrinkled.

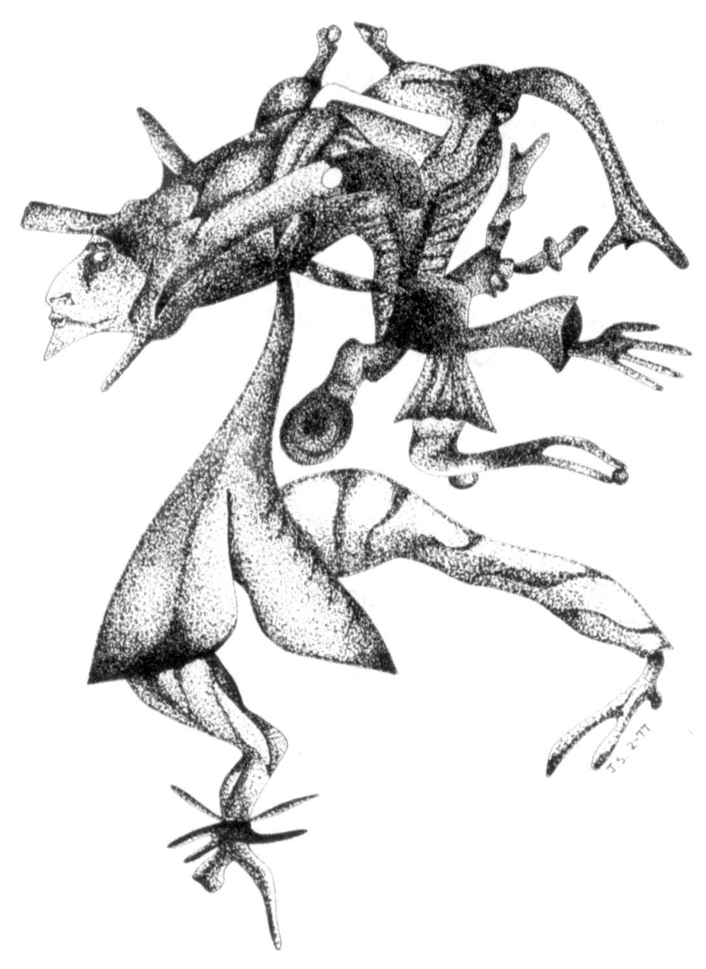

Pointed Toes on Crescent Feet

I

In the turn does one speak
Of pointed toes on crescent feet,
Roots that dust quadratic lines
And show the soft shoe not far behind
Our erecting impulse?

Finally partners are beaten downward
Voices cracked in splitting thought,
Spitting salacious creamy tomes
Within concupiscent crystal domes
Into comic dross.

Of the bean that wrinkled drew
A sign that love for a chosen brew
Will pierce the panicked blanching face.
But no seed can speed the promise of the race
Beyond the bloody cross.

It tugs our faces to the ground
Gapping before the brilliant sound
Of petals dropping before the pier
That holds aloft our corniced fear
The rattle softened by the loss.

II

Will I hold before this weary stump
The petals of a virgin's rump.
Or will I slide upon the wave
And meet the maker in his grave
Of silken thought.

Hold back the confluence
Of her magnanimous dress sutured
On sheets clean and white
The emblem of collective night
Red thread embossed.

The threat assumes a persistent ring.
Ding, the shroud's a ringing thing.
We offered it a song and hoped
For a hard reflection of the trope,
Strong and false.

In the turn does one speak
Of pointed toes on crescent feet?

Is this the love?
Says the virgin orchid,
Unfolding
For the iridescent hummingbird
In the land of woodpeckers.

But was that breathless expression
Also coded like the plumage
And the petals?

Or was the fabric ripped
To unveil an act defiant
Of all the power of the world?

For time you can have a wash of color but no line
To stroke those troughs whose fine intend can hide
Waves to a passing craft to save you from the flood.
Corrected with a lens, the vase will lose its contour
And release the silhouetted face for a moment
To prove that liquid ground can float salvation
As a ring with no attachment, chain or rope, to show
Accompanying direction into prefigured arms.

Practice with no place in particular for urgent kicks,
Looks now deeper into the circle of transparent sea
Teaming with forms not personified by ready fear
And to those bobbing buoys whose bells now sound
Familiar and, crusted with old salts, preserve nothing
Unsung except for all the tales not yet rung for thee.
Weighted, the submerged apparatus will soon sink
The severed sentiment of Captains Courageous
Whose head and arms rest on the unsigned wreath.

Rotten with love,
  the menu soiled, bruised and dog eared,
Offers the enumerated lunchtime specials.
He inevitably chooses number three, no beans,
And a universe beyond the baby numbers.

Crumbled sheets,
  smells like dog and happy tail,
Can be read too, in review, like the meal agenda.
Lacerated souls to justify the secret ambition
Of aimlessness, draped not creased and confused.

What image
  could compete with the garter snakes,
The babies with ancient names and frog legs?
So French, maybe something Italian, a Leopard,
Would bring the adoring blonds to his table.

And would that be a filling of the greedy boy?
Whose spoon would be diminishing greetings
The elaborate holds and secret ingredients,
That hustle in that kitchen beyond the door.

And Reuben went in the days of wheat harvest,
and found mandrakes in the field,
and brought them unto his mother Leah.
Then Rachel said to Leah,
Give me, I pray thee,
of thy son's mandrakes.
דודא

Not just bleeding,
But the slapstick of entanglement,
A pantomime of purpose in stunned intent,
Freezing the rival enterprise mid-stride,
Popping the cake walk win –
This is the assassin's juice:
Enough for one more hit.

Love has reason
To exercise its grandiosity.
Unshackled idols lubricated with saffron,
Spitting forbidden revenge from behind,
Mocking the wormwood sacrifice –
Such is the fornicator's wax:
Endless taper of what remains.

Eyes are itching
For the twilight of conformity.
A dimly fitted room needing no adjustment,
Shelving a book marked midway,
Tracing fingers in the fuzzy dust accumulated –
What is the mediator's line:
Brilliance refracted by the shades.

Fly abstractions
To the mandrake for encumbering
The assets of a caress never budgeted.
Adding neat rows to make ends meet,
Rooting in statistics for a touch invariant –
Here are the accountant's last sums:
Tangibles unbalanced for missing signs.

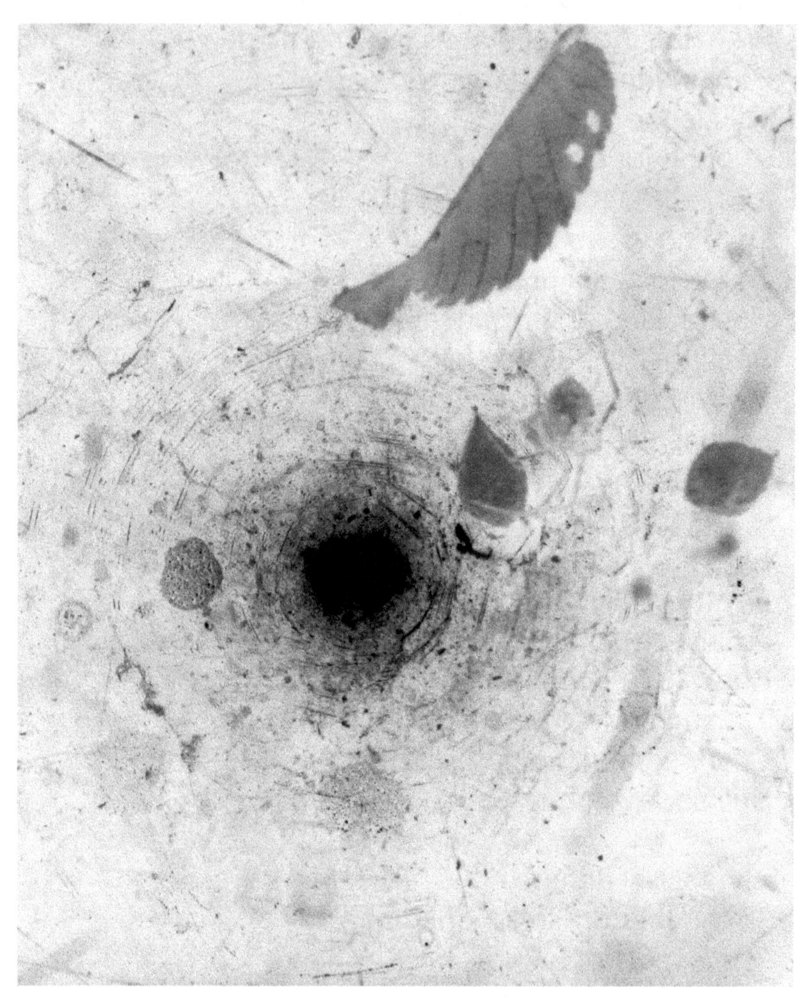

I

Though it had crossed the boundary of reason,
Where the future is generally figured to arrive
Accordingly and within the scope of prediction
Made with the precision of the eight legged spider
Machine, sucking the juice of June bugs in July,
Her finger stretched to feel the pluck of thread
Signaling the arrival of scrawny young men
And other prey that will give service to her
    production –
The minuscule and the many to discover just what
Combinations are appropriate to the place and time,
The figure in flight could not abandon such value
As is found in those misconceived subjectivities
Central to the composition of a web designed
To add little to the emptiness of space and so trap
The excited beetle whose nervous adventure
Precluded the notion that space may be little empty.

II

That all nobility could be rolled was found
To indicate the door to perception was molecular,
Though a confusion of method and content
Gave advantage to mesmerizers, preachers
And idolatrous leaders who might profit
From the opening of doors and implant,
In dark bedrooms, ideologies, utopias and faith.
The sale was a guarantee on the economy of scales.

That the most popular ideas involve singularities,
The god, the star, the unique self,
Armed and righteous, ready for any lurking
    humiliation
Is already so contradictory as to be a mirror
Held at a high angle so as to see the low
Gloriously elevated, or past but conserved
As tribute to a prior enlightenment.
The scandal is not the short, dull vision
Of faith merchants and old men needing young men
To die on the prick of their word,
But the certainty of delusion.

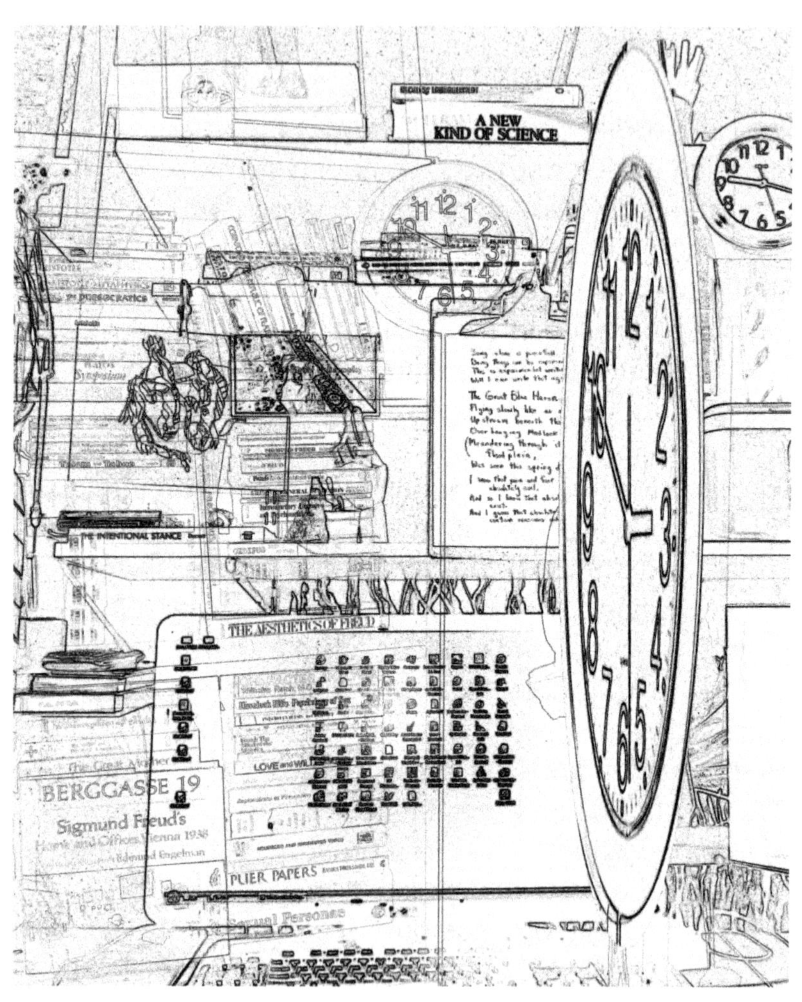

A NEW
KIND OF SCIENCE
THE INTENTIONAL STANCE
THE AESTHETICS OF FREUD
The Great Mother
BERGGASSE 19
Sigmund Freud's
LOVE and WILL

Time has no breadth.

That all the things that were are still in tense
Like a keyword, abridged to pass openings
In narrow threads, a shibboleth to knit
An urgent passage baring tongues too tangled.

The smoke of pipes sequestered in the rooms,
Where tutors nodded not a century
Before to chart the slide of history,
Rises long, attenuated, escaping.

Geometries residing on a pin
Do not infer a cooling vault ahead
In Babylon. Snaking, hanging streets,
The angels' marketplace, is no agora.

And Babel too would make a further point
On polyglot. Many stories to piece
Together higher, graduated fiction
When subplots fall, returned diminished.

Not unpleasant, a fine trajectory,
Long and arcing or short, direct in flight,
The arrows are more slender than the air
To matter, in wide places full of rumor.

We would have one of each rehearsing on the runway
Look up adoringly from the forest's mossy floor
And reveal the secret of a scent that cannot be affixed
Exactly to a place, yet seems emitted from a source
More perfect than the tropes following in its wake.

Rag tag, it was written, is played on those exotic sites
In cities where the gamin congregate to exchange
Impressions of the seriously denuded recent kings
Of a budding trend now checkered and even pocked
By burlesque and a laugh from those who would touch.

Never again the silky clay of that finely molded face
Will be stroked. The waving hand of those desires
That only mourn will soon relinquish its grasping hold
On star lit bodies unlike its own and curl into a cramp
Of scorn for fighters in the arenas of its heavy thumb.

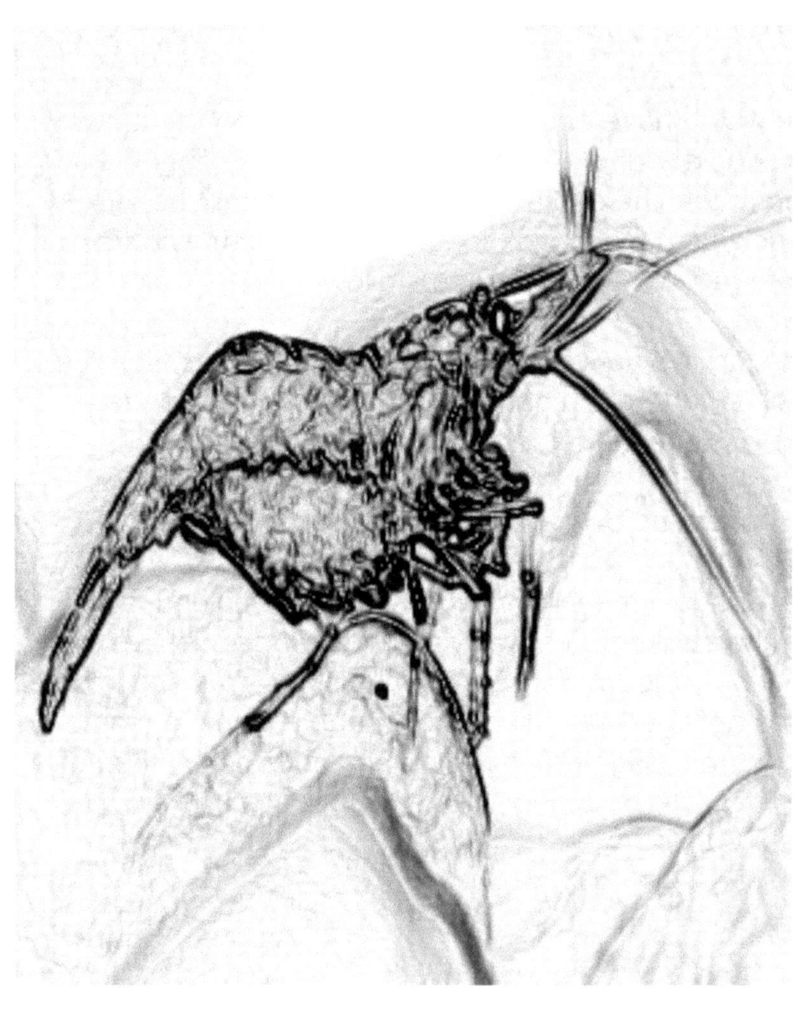

Tales of ghost shrimp prancing through the tank
Or diving, darting, flying, with tail slapping
Horizons like a Moby Dick of lesser rank,
Are measured by the simple meter of mere tapping.

Transparent they have found the hiding place
Most perfectly protected from the eye balls
Of back boned hunters in the finny race
Who glide among the feeding phantoms culling.

For a meal will betray and so will sex
As these are dark things hidden inside.
Target spots for marauding hunger vexed
By light and shades with color not applied.

Thus not secured against adverse encounters
Permanently, these hollow spirits form
Dainty souls, pairs of feet mounting
The marathon stage, dancing for the unborn.

Empty souls with haunting skill but few plans,
Have tiny forks for eating snails half grown.
What else but indigestion halts the dance
Of undulating flaneurs at the Bois de Boulogne?

Beguile your watered rhyme with a snap and a flip.
Ghost shrimp are unseen until you dip.

Write in the morning, edit in the afternoon,
While the blankness lets you know that the brain
Actually exists but beyond the apprehension,
Like, Like, Dillinger's prick in a pickle jar.

What about that girl in the red dress
And the unscripted climax that followed
Her every move with an economy that foretold
The profitless future. Let it go. Sell now.

A creature swims the warm and salty sea.
That is its substance, not the fin and ripples
Of the flimflam logic that would so prove
Singularities and consistencies abundant.

Mythologies awaken on the empty shore
And soon enough are dressed to serve
At the function, whose attraction mainly rests
On the narration of a chosen sequence.

She at any rate had already given her honors
And needed but a composition that would prove
Her conclusion. Fumbled scraps and pieces,
Broken leads, leaky pens, and little time

To begin: The great general Horace never
Faded away nor rode his horse beyond the river.

The first lines bemoaned alone of course:
“It is an old, old man who tells this tale,
Though he is but eighteen summers past.”
Something, something that rhymes with tale.
“The years have traveled years too fast.”

Not quite right but certainly better.
And so on among the creeping vines.
Then the wand was raised and waved
And the kindly teacher Cleghorn
Forgave grammar and encouraged verse:

“Hey Harvester pull that plough,
So that I graciously endowed
Can be shoveled a heap of manure
And buried in dirt my soul to pure.”
And so advanced the appropriated life --

To a sad song for a coffee house and this joke:
“Behind my ear she nibbled,
Ecstasy never stops,
A mosquito’s foil can riddle,
Man’s most tender thought.”

Ah, the complete oeuvre like frogs
Have jumped from their box.

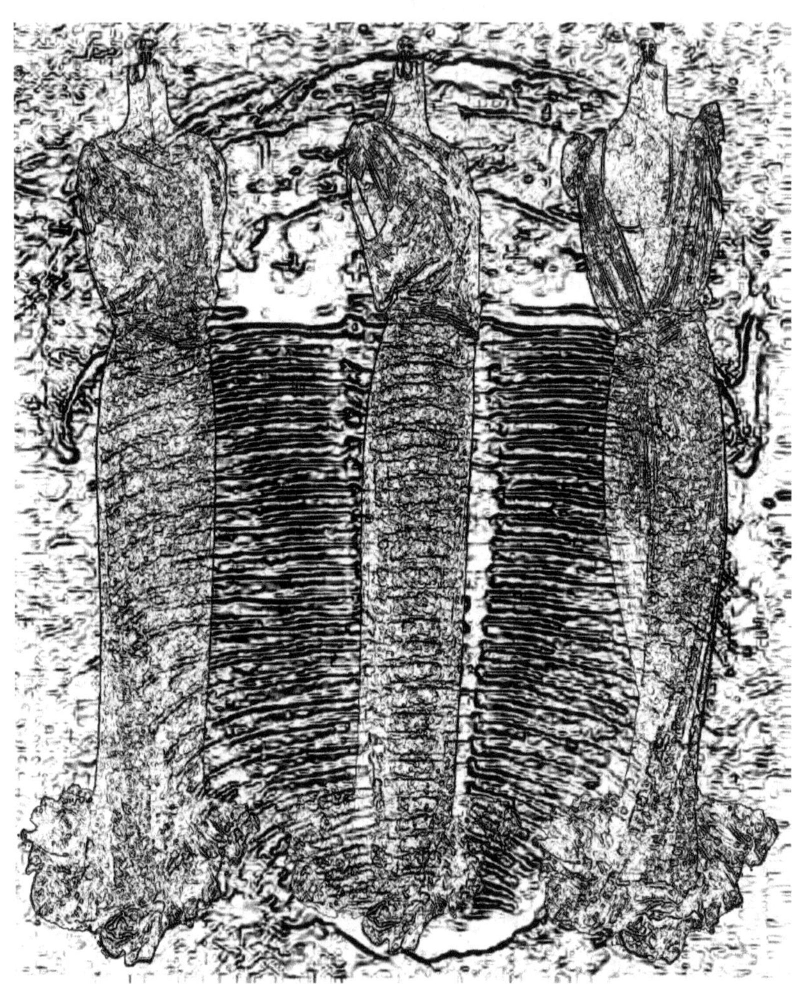

Look at that spider out the window.
Does it frighten you? Focus your powers.
You, a man lively with cobwebs and dust,
Cannot destroy it with your X-ray vision.

Self maintaining and carefully aware,
You have received unauthorized sensations,
From the inner god whose zealousness
Is grape cool aid and sweet deceit.

Did you pass the acid test
Within you and without you,
The fizz of those carbonaceous critters
Whose chronicles encode obliteration?

Did you think that inside the bone
True marrow and essential cores would guide
Form and pattern like the draped flesh
So admired for your minutes alone?

Thinking, weights and measures, a dry chapter,
Unlike judging, you say? What fits together
Some more enduring assemblage named Everfresh
With the concrete image of her tiny offspring.

Egg balls are prepared according to the menu
Enhanced by fractions of secreted silk,
Until they disappear and lost children,
Hang hungry about the gallows and debris.

The truly desperate have raised their cry and died
And left behind, for a while, the mainly civilized
Stragglers whose skill makes use, instead of words,
Of signs to build well placed deeds or just enormity.

Would the opening, that same one Being there,
Have waited anyway without a wary soul to charm?
Waited, perhaps, for the lazy and bored nobility
To turn rash justice into knowledge as fine as lace.

What but so long as yesterday is nicely baked,
Served with apple metaphor so science may feed
The hungry savage -- if the taste would be acquired.
But rectitude in used book stores does not ripen.

Once you have done them several times, the leaps
Beyond some current reason adopt a place
In the thumbed catalog somewhat after women's
Underwear, not that you were not unscarred.

Tattooed with raised and pinkish tissue to record
The accumulated negatives used just before to fill
And ward off a seeping abscess felt beneath the hair.
There you go again on Lincoln's birthday with a play.

To mold that face into a personality and mask,
Concave, and therefore really Being there. To gaze
It has the opening slit and some repertoire of pain
Or fear to perform in a clearing once lit by fire.

Once or twice they played with paper dolls and girls.
Carefully cutting out and bending tabs to fashion endless
Wardrobes stuffed with more better design
To collect, like rocks or stamps, the one world.

Most average girls, pretty and assured at early age
Of their grave ability to swiftly change any given moment
With inviting smiles and chirps, played the game
More socially, and so honed with practice their edge.

The boy though he knew the giggle did not know
The language and perceived it thus as pricking nibbles,
Foreign bodies like thorns and splinters. His to protrude
Into the closet scene, yet seem not, or be stabbed.

They stripped the Muslim men to reveal humiliation
And unlocked the overlapping plates that guarded solitude
The torturers knew so well but thought unworthily
Having secretly played with girls on rainy days.

Coming
ice?
STADO Y MOLIDO PARA EL BUST
BUST
ESCAFEINA
SIEMPRE FRESCO,

Udder eyes, what? To see reminders on the fridge
Of the tongs and blocks of ice needed to preserve
Verisimilitude. Some bloody spots on hallow ground
Will dew for any idea that would otherwise translate.
And this is the battle ground, this daily grind,
For scores in bed, on stage, it's just
   The old homestead.

Caught, crunched, forked and pinned,
   discovered naked,
Rape it. But that all wet Jason, you know,
   just won't fry.
So continue the torture and turn inside out like a worm
Making his way home through the burrow of greasy,
Grimy, gopher guts to the holy captured wormlita
Who will squirm and giggle open the other end.

And lo again. The September sun has just the slant
To justify desiccation. "So why not"? as they say,
Who say in coffee bars where the countless spoons
Nod in recognition to the cup of being there unstirred.
Oh yea and no wonder they would chose an essay
To nail the red queen and snuff the mad hatter.

A place so strange that Father Abraham
Was lost. The light of moral reason dimmed,
Dissolved. Rebellions staged in frozen black
Dismembered priest hoods repeating chants
Urging comfort onto the gravely dead.

Some words unaltered by the reach for warmth
Or gold may stay behind to guard the breech,
Heckled into solemnity and truth,
The stones of life, but not the fetish bone,
Waggled before the body's gaping pit.

A hacked but clever pile arranged to swear,
Revenge and damn, the swarm of careful thought
Will not avert the stinger bright and sharp
That bites beneath its tough preserving hide
Expelling bile to justify some truth.

But just is that aligned to follow not
Exactly so along the riddled wall –
To creep and bob and still make covenant
Now in this seeping place of foreign birth
We are stranger here among the tools divine.

The little weasel trapped inside still tries to gnaw
It's way out as if it could not imagine permanent
Imprisonment running Master's spinning wheel
Forward then backward in the sweet bony room.

With night visitors he will conspire to escape.
They say they have heard of him and want him
For the program of history probably, he thinks
And suggests for privacy they step into the hall

Of halls not painted pea soup green but modern
Eyed with lap top dancing and coffee shop displays
Of goodies paralyzed for a view incorporated.
The bearded man from history has noticed

The excellence of the weasel work so far done.
But he, like substance, begins to fade into the noise
That wiggles its way through the smallest hole,
Its interference pattern suggesting desperation.

For recruits will manage the texts and file the paper
Shreds while smallish creatures manufacture disdain
Or flattery and so get to ooze into the copy room
Of naked girls who catch the weasel using gloves.

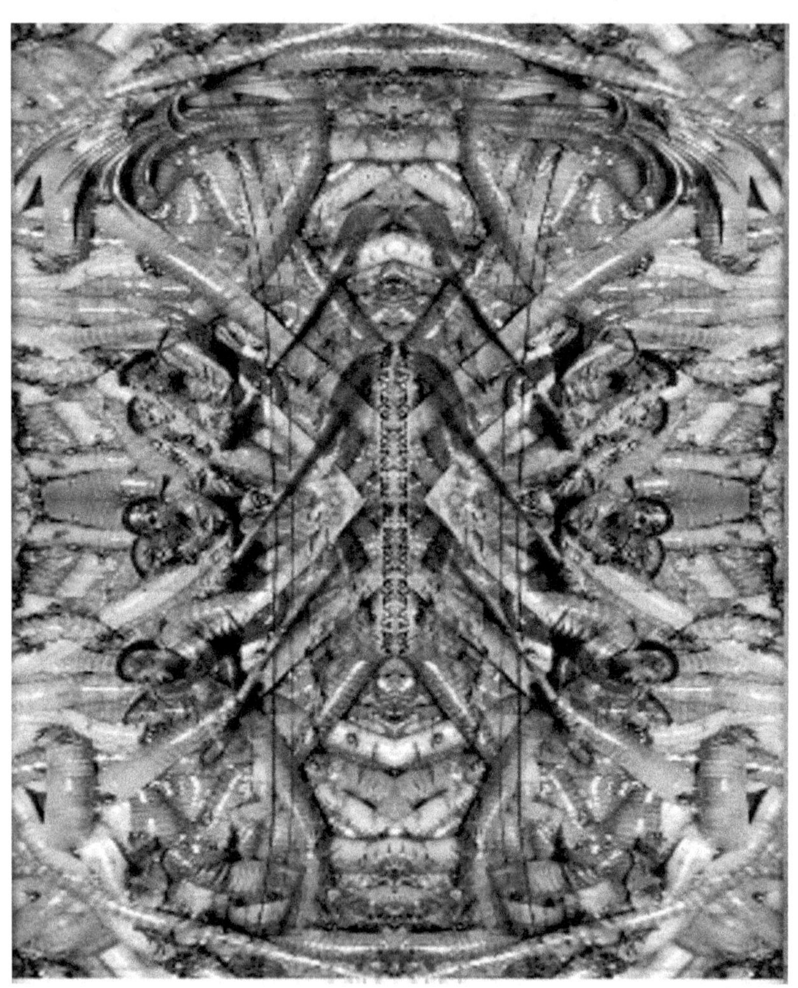

The remembered events had no plot or even drama.
How could they as they were then seemingly open
Only to the desultory action inhabited not yet seen
Flatly from a distance as are characters on a stage.

Only in their second life as the remembered image
Do they form the tableau and then gather force
To project their selves toward some fatality:
The cathartic proof bred from unbroken reasoning.

One could make a story for any scene or ink blot.
Once it has been given the face of symmetry
It will march triumphant on a sandstone arch
Over the heads of all the fallen monuments.

What movement was there on the flattened estuary
The gunnels of the stillborn rowboat greased
By globs and pieces of congealed worm and eel
The bait hung over, lead weighted and waiting.

Waiting for fish, father, author to end the futility
Of that luckless day. Waiting to passively capture
The sequestered bounty beneath the flat bottom.
Waiting so as not to quit and feel the wrath.

Undisturbed by the slightest breath, each mote
Though just, still rises through the streaming sunlight
Knocked about, no doubt, by some heated molecule.
Or is it itself the most smallest thing, a name
Tweezed from the alphabetic galaxy of future orators.
Baby Breath and yelps otherwise that flourish
Will not induce the plume to sacrifice its indolence
To a rolling direction, the vector of a vague desire,
Until the technique, almost a whistle, is mastered.
Other tricks to come, like dancing on your hind legs,
Will obliterate the memory of a lazy day in genesis
Now made measureless by the tick shuffling history's
Simple rules into gospel towers, tall and breathless.

A Ramshorn dropped into the acrylic city
From the palm of retired curiosity,
Is now insured by those transparent walls,
Its policy more permanent and immune
To invasive risk than any single thing
Of flesh, shell or bone could sign.

Who would say the recurved surface
Was not infinite?
Molluskan nomads making way across
The smooth plane exchange elements,
Gamble on rich transmutations,
Successive dissipations, random genuflections.

Yet if this container world is sealed
So final and tight that the constricted scream
And its smiling daughters are only claims
Recorded for a recount of the sum,
Then why are the larval forms,
Unsigned, awaiting signatures?

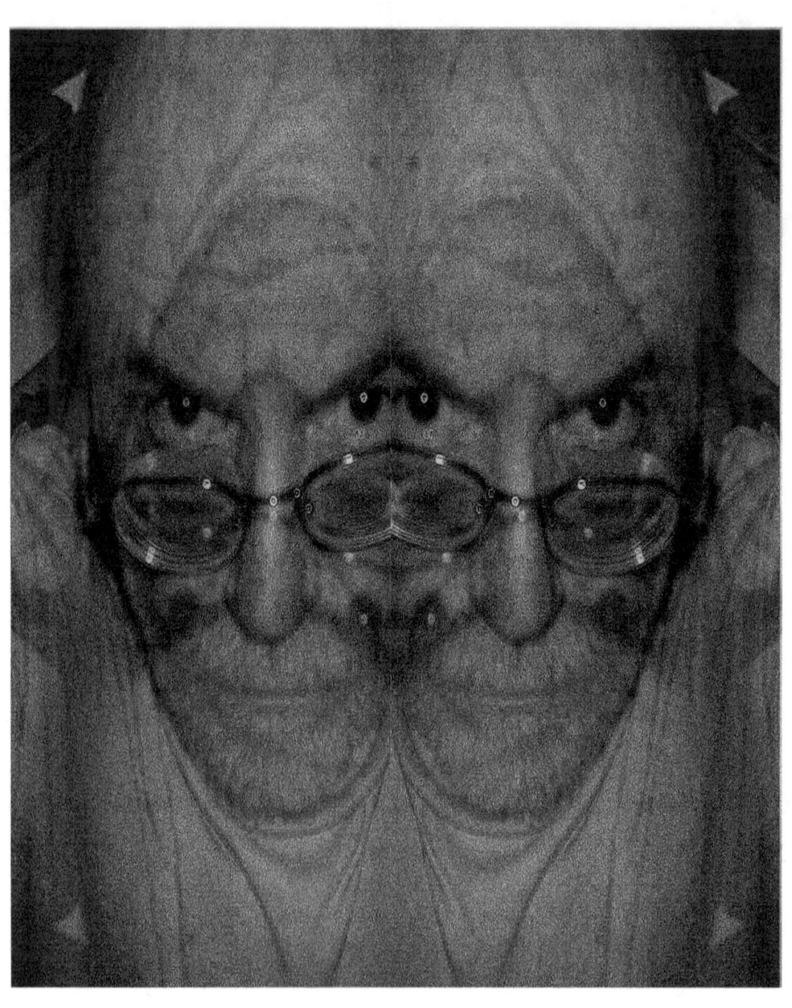

I

This man barely sown,
Ass crack above his belt,
Nose a bubbling mass,
Asymmetrical in every way,
Wanted to get ahead.

His wife was at home with cancer.
What a con.
But who would say no to misery
Even after the accumulated
Minutes after minutes,
Of having watched.

Through alimentary conveyance,
Through the laser glory hole,
Profit sweetened patrons,
Got their dose,
Having fumbling intercourse
With their pockets
Before the evening shows.

All-Bran
Original
FAGE
Total 0%
Velveeta
Original

II

And he chatted about
Her colostomy bag:
The nurses, orderlies,
Would not clear the tubes,
And has anyone really seen
A doctor lately,
And would not empty the bag,
So what to do?

Chocolate frozen yogurt
Is melting in the cart
As his big melon made its way
To the small brown
Imported fingers
Checking the commercial pulse,
Soon to be replaced, replaced, replaced . . .

Let me take these out for you sir,
Said the white,
Potato girl, Spud,
Studded with an eager eye,
Sensing all natural advantage
Over the cynically dead.

With the varied schedule of rewards,
The scientist had him beat again, methodically.
The difficulty of shocking this old guy
Into wiggling his toes comes from corroded anodes.
Solutions can be autoclaved, or even half baked,
To regen the lost molecules, marbles, bearings,
Balls of steel, so queer, quilty and queeg.

And would that be justice: to set once more
The triumphal entry into the city,
Her city, any back lot city, like Ben Heracles?
Or was it the eternal missing heart of nature
That left him so morose?

When the watchers check his notebooks,
Watching for their recognition,
Will they notice the data slightly altered?
Few will have their watchers.
Those that do gather all the better glory
And birdseed. (to me, to me, to me).

Is not all the point
And pinnacle of review
But how not to disdain lovers,
Or fake the knowing of a view,
Or worship the layered shades,
Or expect one more assignation
In the wilderness traversed.

He gives us rum and adventures rarely now
But Diablo Dub Loon, cockeyed captain
Of our beloved barge, the Lady Lap Light,
Can still spin a yarn if you wind him upright.

Have you heard the one about old Sid,
Tied to a wooden horse and though dead,
Led the charge against the Trodden Women.
At the feast he ate his mom in a drunken moment.

Or George the Buckaroo who cleaned the stables
In far off Ba Buddha Land. They say his mouth
Could launch a thousand ships but was too tight
For Ahab to dock his wackin' white cheroot that night.

They danced, played and loved the sunny view.
Pigeon plump piazzas served corn.
Scaled feet traced pilgrims through
Portals framing shrines to saints reborn.

The hoary king chewed his Proverbs well.
So cunning bakers powdered Hell in bowls,
Mixed letters so vaulted Age could spell
The chapter next, the Word of rage foretold.

A hundred billion cells collapse as one
Before the fountain rimmed with murmuring.
The plastered cupids dip their rays in sun
To aim at falling days their furthering.

With slow measure the ancient feet can walk
The staggered stations across the cobbled talk.

Would such perfection in stroking,
That grooms the emulation of all,
Those with sprung excrescences,
And those smooth as a peeled egg,

Those who still imagine that the locust
Are benign and well fed grasshoppers
Overflowing with sweet grass, those engorged
With littered stardust and labile signs,

And those still busy ants and flies,
Who would abduct the Not Is, Was Is,
And other mad teapot Philosophies Pupal,
From plates seasoned by ancestor chefs,

Divert the sleeping dog,
Floating in his chair,
From dreaming tail wagging gulps
Of beefy boy and horsey chow?

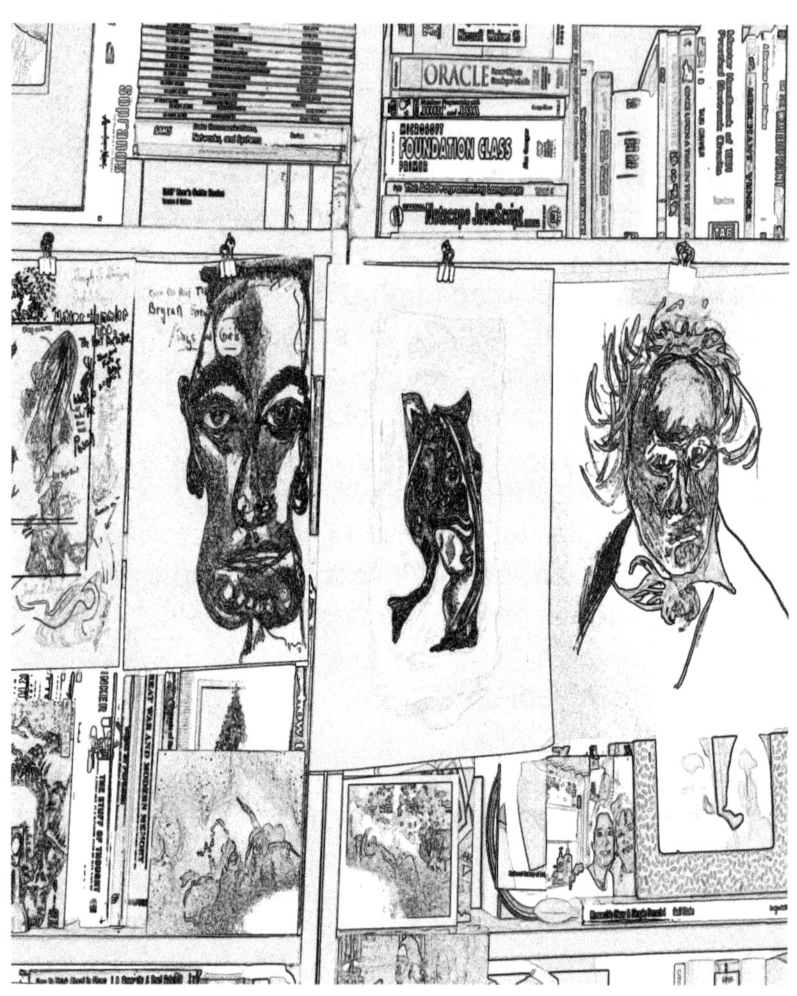
ORACLE
MICROSOFT
FOUNDATION CLASS
PRIMER
The Ada Programming Language
Netscape JavaScript
SAMS
Data Communications, Networks, and Systems
THE STUFF OF THOUGHT
GREAT WAR AND MODERN MEMORY

I

Who would do it again and again,
Chained to the floor, with just enough
Freedom to put meat before the master
And lick clean the after dinner plate
To soothe a salt inveigled hunger?

Pieces on the floor of imagination
May convince the supplicant more sharply
Than what is known not far above,
Where lumbering ancestors dispense
Wit or outrage to chisel notches.

Below the table boards, the checker board,
The lowly dreamers arrange the scraps,
Proving the conversation a sacred act,
A legend around the carving circles,
A chalice filled with hash and eggs.

II

Now where is Uriah Heep?
You need him to butter the lamb
And fuck your purse with cringing metaphor.
Push, push for some result and what comes
But chatter and chicken scratch.

Where is the grain from last year
Harvested to be sown this spring?
Now a dried and bitter feast unshared,
And so it was in the beginning,
Nausea, Sartre hell of other people.

Masters and slaves . . .
Cooked realities . . .
Enlightened barnyards . . .
Fruitless creation . . .
The fallen goods.

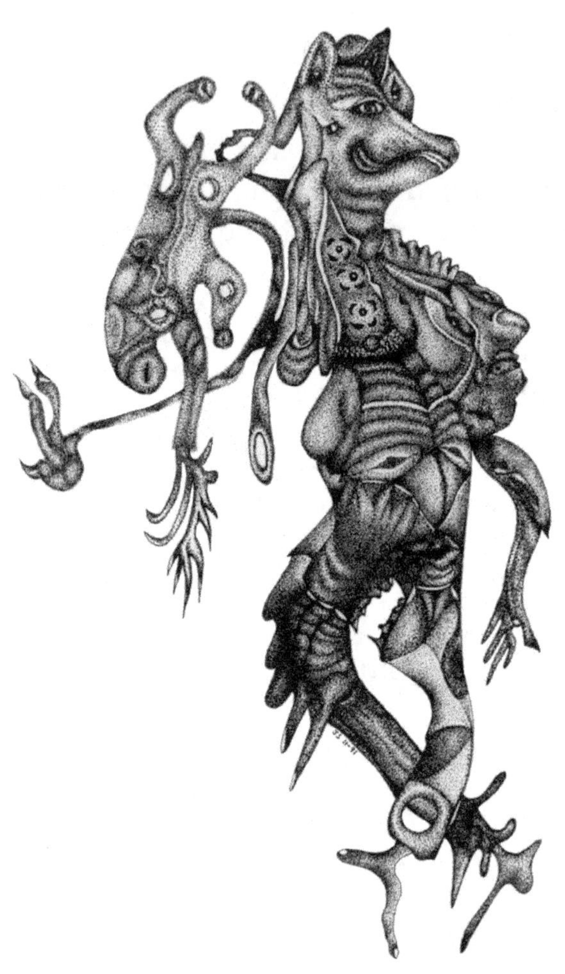

Appreciated for a craft that seemed inbred with nature,
Dimwit deliberated his lines, clotted, barely heard,
A gurgled continua for the nebula of new lit stars,
A collapsing chant for union troopers and journeymen.

False humility is no less true, unless comedy is not
A profession for mimics who pry with levers an image
Like certain moths and butterflies of something large,
Distasteful to those clever few hoisted by the yarns

Of Madame Guillotine who will chronicle the event
Methodically, with balance and a critical needle,
Of moderate size that though eyeless is still glinting
While the players shuffle on the boards to speak

Of far, far greater things beyond the scaffolding
Where court is held on the inner things of Dimwit
King whose muttering is not yet cut by Direction
So inverse reflection will rehearse a sparse attendance.

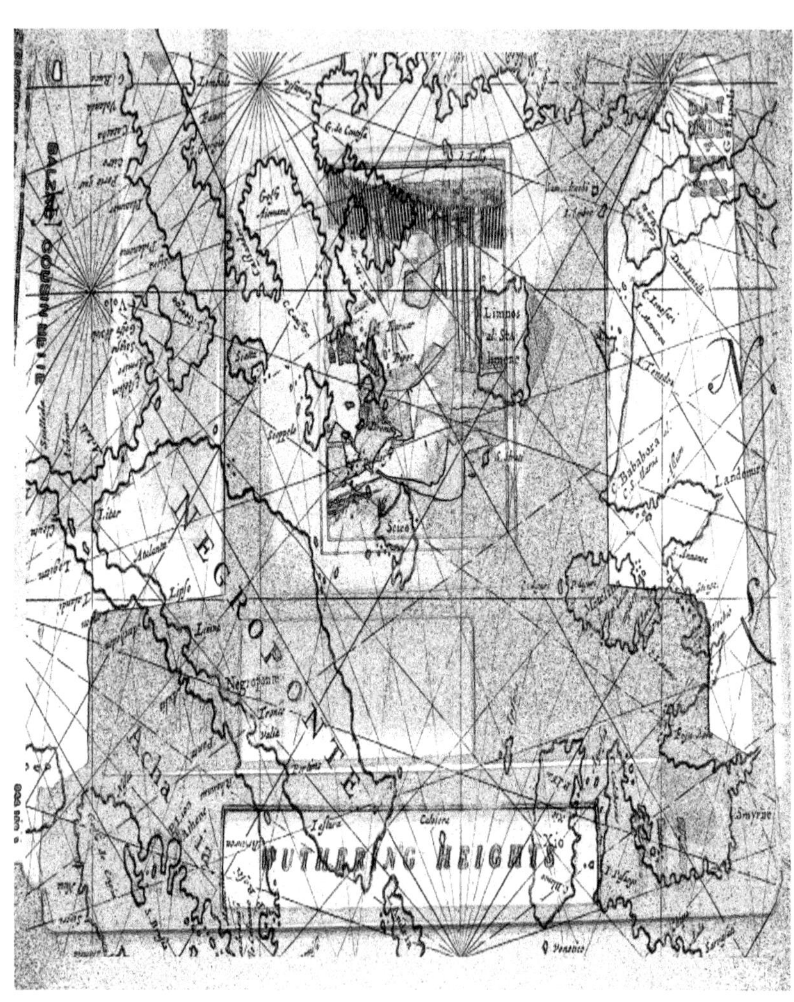

WUTHERING HEIGHTS
NEGROPONTE
Negropont
Limnos
Scio
Smyrne

When angels were the arm of God, what silly man
Struggled in the dust and held the imagined line
Recording its role in each night's epic tale --
Cooked up after a day of wandering and goating.

The original string theory would begin to unravel
Late afternoon before the camel was created,
As heads nodded toward the cool urn of sleep
And the chants began to take an edge best avoided.

Just so it served prolongation of walking erections,
That, like the tale, anticipates its own sequester,
Behind a comic faith that beguiles a coming falter
Of narration, smarmy hops and hot summer salted.

The righteous are obedient hypocrites and idiots,
But then who is not once or twice too good,
Too indignant and too sated on a moral issue?
They will treat you fairly well even if you cross
Them once or twice to deal in broken legacies.

Papa has a good word for you when you're back
In gear, out on bail, accountant for the big bank,
Your multicolored coat neatly belted in the middle.

You once or twice knew a baby baboon on TeeVee
Who ate bananas, poked and tickled, giggled.
She wore a diaper but still lifted up her skirt
Jungle style, for the stunt that must follow:
The clapping seal, eating fish, juggling beach balls.

This act would soon make way for the inside dope:
Aggression, territory, teeth and social hierarchy,
Captured for real, imprinted on reels by lanky Jane.

Until you hate all, the sentiment, tough critter,
Will be live. You cannot pick and choose an ark
Or channel but once or twice before deeper sympathy
For each thing breaches the thin ocean surface,
Splinters the vessel, making shards of rectitude.

For Robert and Claire

A ghost unchallenged slips through rooms of wit,
Is netted gently by brimming glasses gazing --
By amber tears and windows dimly lit,
By passing beams that worry tavern phrasing.

Chilled ground dampens rippled remorse,
A homeless hour for Hermit's homeless grief.
Burnished idols along our liquid course
Reflect a burial beneath the litter and the leaf.

Loss rolled, descends an overwhelming hill.
Or tossed, will come again to juggled lives.
Who sits this out and waits to pay the bill?
Who cranks a somber organ, who strokes the vibes?

A cheer for thickened lips and staggered gait,
Those drinking deep who rising, snag the bait.

Tool Options
CHAPTER 1
In search of style
they normally get up in the morning
and do not stop talking to family
and friends all day long, etc.

The article said they normally get up in the morning
And do not stop talking with relatives and friends
All day long. Now this is a foreign race that spits
Food and debates philosophies over bathroom stalls.

Spending time together – and what else can be spent
Or bought for all that matters in a brief forever –
Serves as goodness for the domestic safe and sane
Whose charted course is fairly marked and centered.

But those whose pivot has not been set and drifts
Across the maps, from sheet to sheet then back,
Seeking the lost impression of an imagined self,
Are also fluent aliens in continuous conversation.

When age once keenly gathered no longer creeps,
And wife or mother would find a listener more adept,
And all others, but dogs, are increasingly practical,
The insanely lonely talker finally will inscribe.

Confessionals are darkly made,
The lattice works to diffuse
The naked, jagged line to demonstrate
Not all is light redressing matter.
After thoughts betray
Both tentative thrusts
And jots he boldly played.

With a finger move the dust
To round and blend and merge
Hither thither destruction
Applied to greater wholes
And outer shells just recognized.
In caves the justifying nod
Evokes a sleepy silhouette.

Why is it that everyone else
Is so good or so self
Consciously bad that his little sin
Of mediocrity, or less, or lease,
Must obscure the indolent line,
And Heckle and Jeckle
Are the menace of his time?

What habit once raised by tango steps,
Feathers, drugs and movie snips could fire
Volcanic fakery and ignite the bedroom sky?

Banana hats and taro leaves are lips,
Expanding too rapidly at thirty frames
A clip, to catch a glimpse of naked thigh.

Come drops, rain shields your darkened clouds,
Shrieking cinder wings revenge the sprout
Of snake children caught sulfuring the pitch.

The feast of soup uneaten still profits.
It trades in bits of tantalizing kin forgotten.
Steel can serve for silver spoons eloping.

Exact reflections deep in darker ponds
Unveil the fallacies corrupting ageless time
Of shimmering youth and scripts dimensionless.

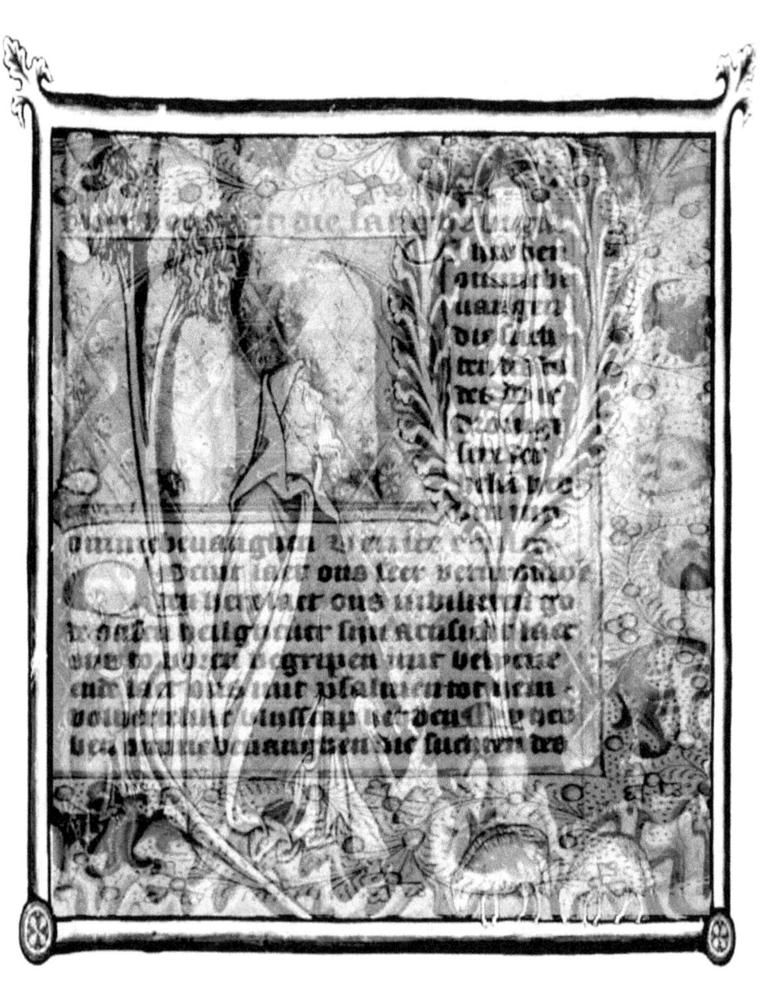

I

Yahweh would surely say to Moses:
Your flattery suggests you do not know
I am who I am even on Saturday night
Or by the burning light of your humility.

Well maybe not so roundly
But with a snaky finger shot
Straight through the stutter hole
To the small callous of his stubborn soul.

The punk stood whining dis-connections
To elder dons, to Abraham, Issac, Jacob.
Adrift? So much the better, for magic snakes
And spells increase the protection racket take.

la cupe ioseph est troue en le sac beniamin.

le filz iacob unt amene iacob en egyp a ioseph.

II

And God said:

Now, as holy ground is forbidding lost,
But horny monsters hunt down your virtue,
The twisted halls of shrinking compass,
Suggest a valediction to Egyptian turf.

Your common mothers seduced by roots
Clapped together the family myth
Of precious Joseph, lost to violent gangs,
Who returned again to save the lawless youth.

Finally God said to Moses:

No hurt can be imagined
To endlessly cure itself.
Books accumulate tissue.
Let scars be your wealth.

I

The riddle of the dried peas that rattle
In Jack's head will not be solved
Convincingly with monkish chants or preachers
Conducting shrieks, snakes and drumming.

They don't require a deceiving beard,
Doctored exhortations unfolding secrets,
The butt ends figured yesterday
By ragged claws and smoking cats.

Awe precedes the stake not plunged
In streams. Refracted roots derive
Coordinates of first attempts to clear
An opening, answers to drowned being.

Reflecting tension, the confining skin
Offers entry to the sticking pin
That spots escaping ills defined
By poison droplets boiled in fear.

Approved by capital freely hung,
Chattel passing word will choose
Overseers insured by bloody spikes
And snapping whips that whistled pain.

A nickle and a dime for visions down
The line, of transparent futures
Sold short in market optimism,
And passing gates guarding death.

II

One sound for torrents to Joseph's two,
Intruders do not escape the ford.
The wading children ill pronounced,
Mince phrases in stuttered fear.

They bet with time to beggar places,
Collecting alms for tortured limbs,
They trade the promised flood of wealth
For blistered secrets and phantom pain.

Propelled behind the ancient force
Of flagellation crafting dread,
Engraving writers sign their tombs:
A river crossed, the other death.

In wood the storming fingers less precise
Enlighten deeply the face of random love.
But brier worts resist the craving knife,
The threaded press, the bed and sheet above.

Preferring lamplight to hanging friends,
We hear the chorus chant of heavy snow.
They find crevasse, avalanche, a morning freeze,
In stacking wood and knuckle bones they throw.

The breath goes now or no, from common view
Unseen, measured by arc and pendulum.
From wooden planks Notus tossed the crew
To mutiny, turquoise bays and tropic rums.

The Gothic printer matched growth to grain
The palms are gone, the compass arms retained.

Sweating out the last chemical attack?
The clammy due clings to your rubber suit.
Prisoner of your own army and blanket gas,
Frantic command structures strut in circles,
You squat hormonal by the wet and ruined bed.

The dome of calculation's higher law,
Besieged by salty waves and raining toads,
Fashioned thickly by masons, marbled to endure
Insulting gulls and pecking magpies,
Bequeaths a rhyming tide and sandy beach.

Furrows plowed through ardent rock,
Collapse the barrel vaults protecting envy.
Your jealousy paces exposed to roaring storms,
As the laughing harem paddles carelessly away
With all the winking pearls of vice you gave.

Secret treasures, resentment's sour wine,
Sealed so long in caves and counting rooms
By chiseled doors that feign your pious heart
Or your indifference concealed by love of art,
Drift in currents, exposed, their pulse uncorked.

The guards, ran off with pretty things,
Old rarities securely chained and booked,
Adornments are streaming out the scuppers
Of the sinking castle you thought anchored.
Your flags are drenched in brine and oozing color.

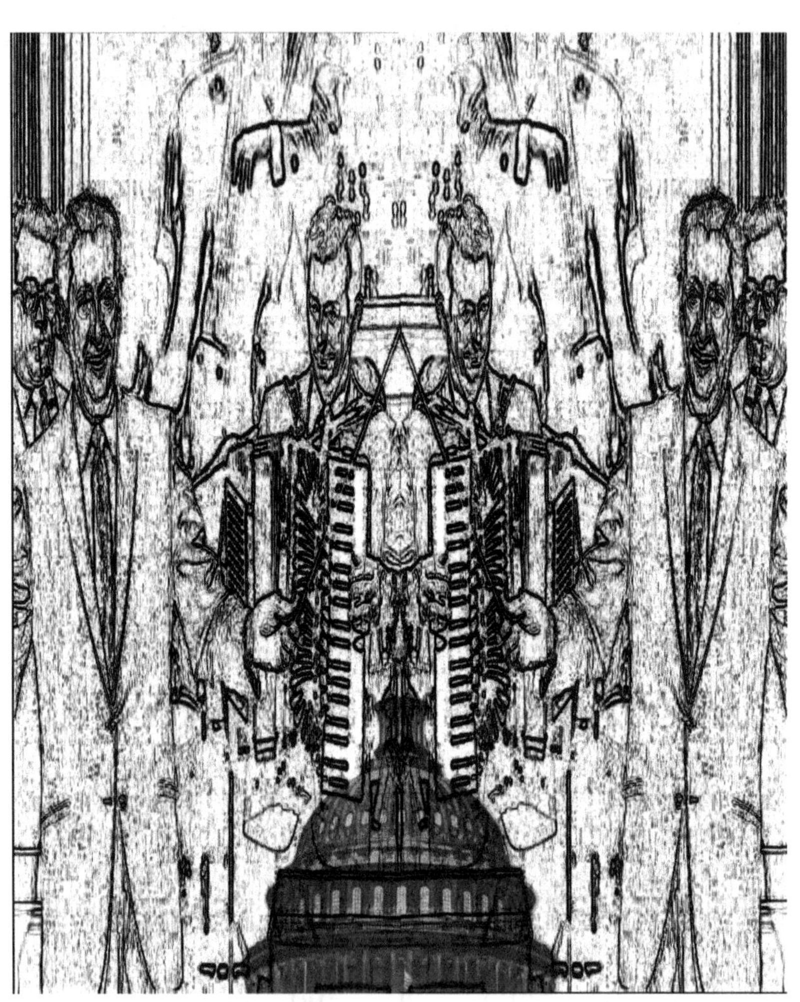

The tunes that play in parliament, strummed
On banjos and sung with augmented twangs,
Are not performed to make the round melodious.
Such easy pieces call for an arching wand,
Dictating entry time and duplication of accord.

Perhaps the lords will not hear debate among
The nucleated choir opening with ancient music
To prove ancestral claims on the last remains
Of dungeons and country places, their estates.
The clamor is too old for the rubbed bench.

Tiring, now nodding, soon fidgeting with tips,
Tenons, tables, beak and double reeds,
The children of the back row, mouthpiece cleared,
Wait to introduce their plain melody above
The chordal din of second fiddles reproducing.

If a march will sometime bring a new arousal
So domesticated love disembarks for exotic ports
To repeat in confidence the graceful fingering
Of a fugue transcribed for stadium horns,
Tin drums, firecrackers and beating sticks,

Would it but be a place remembered once again,
A warming tonic, the coziness of tones to come.
For chaotic bands in congress misconducted,
A meditative pause, a soundless breath regained,
Pleads to members and beseeches this august body.

There are collections of collections neatly framed
By the glimpse you caught one day below the headlines.
They show their affirmation for the unquiet pause
That aspires to whip the savages into hauling lines.

Still you want a knotted wit that will hardly touch
And turn heads but some modest degree to your hand.
Smile sweet Oliver you withheld the impulse to pillage
On the other hand like Dodger and saw the rise

Of a longer finger whose palm almost transparent
Held a coin that seemed not to barter for position
With the commodity of lint rolled in Fagin's pocket.
But more like porcelain keeping liquid in place.

People frozen near summits,
Have been seen with their hair
Waving on the mountain's wind.
Adventurers see them as they stride
Toward the accomplishment at the top:
Monuments to defeat and braved adversity.

But are they, deep in solitude, having thoughts
Coldly coagulated in their time catching memorials,
About the enduring ending of their past heroic works?
The accumulated details drifting behind them still
Are carved by forces finer than a thunderbolt
Though no less sprung from envy.

So that even in monkeydom
The chatter of fundamental
Charges, tracks in clouded
Chambers and whispers
In the dark are signed
By contemplation.

Possible figures grandly paraded
Then dug under to insure against
Parodies anticipated,
Like copy rite infringements,
Theft of delicate material,
Flights of cawing puns,
And shorter fictions self imposed.

As if the universe had attention
Like a wounded animal
For entrails falling behind
Its plan of continuous action.
Or intention to rub away
The skin, plant tumors for spring,
Like bulbs among the blades.

Aligned along the quiet field,
Markers and their faded script
Would make the dowsing rod suspect
The hidden source so fluent.
In sentiment of common measure,
In work that struck the proper arc
The filigree of iron still frames.

The trading company declined the application.
Fearing more his vicissitudes than corruption,
Which, after all, is tractable with double entry,
It found he would be god to any good or evil
And wanted a monopoly for the foreign post.

Well not exactly. The narrative was garbled
By the late appearance of that famed actor
Who, adopting little Dolores could now diddle
The cellulose revisions of his childish lust
To touch the last remaining nipple nubby.

Chris Craft stained mahogany can grimace,
Yawl, pitch and roll to blue eyed paradise
Arousing the juicy sentiments of desert folk,
To recreate the hit it made just last year
Tortured and buggered by the vicious Turk.

Brigitte Bardot was caught once on the late,
Late show, her tube snuggled almost in bed,
And like her molested mink she's still around
To finish off the narrative scheme of boys
Steaming up streams, overhung, being hooked.

Not far above the project the air yet undisturbed
By the rising heat and dusty noise of friction
Awaits the fluxion of an industry more precise.
The smokestacks dutifully puffing dim clouds
Now this, now that shape prophetic of the wind
Are being plugged like the memorial cannon
On statehouse lawns of wars righteously lost.

Molecular philosophies will re-inter the colors
Seeping from the sulfurous cracks of oracles
In yellow blots on filter paper to solve the riddle
Of inheritance generally valid but not general.
Finally to release the monkey from being more
Then his natural right to chatter of the universe
The relaxing breath will rise through uncluttered air.

That we like Shakespeare in common verse
Could compare is unlikely. Shortness teases
And we will shout the beat two timed worse,
Striving to complete a pretty tune to please.

But pleasure massed and scaled still requires
Applying night, that naught that plies a thought
From sense, the light that works on day's desire,
To wrap, tap and slap the fetal insult.

Confinement self imposed and freely padded
Avoids baboons we fear will bite and steal
Away the juicy fruit of self, or gnats
Denying inner time with mighty deals.

The social cause embeds a stranger dream
Rehearsing empty night, commerce schemes.

Expressions easily reside on a face,
Like the semaphores in Hornblower's day,
They look to move events, forestall invasions,
Declare a state of affairs and promote action.

The code is mingled thought, emotion, feeling,
And is reliable even when broken.
Still the message is a show of fiction,
A ruse learned long ago to please demand.

To move others is not to move oneself as much.
And even if the self is moved, it is as another –
The state having preceded the invocation
Tears like pennies are drops of economy.

The will remembered hard desire arose
In blinkered episodes repeating themes.
Ensuring tides once bore to harbored coves
Embedded riddles proving borrowed scenes.

The resurrections come and go less now.
The canceled play rehearses shows each night,
When mother Mary reads in gossip how
Her plunging neckline requires a knife.

The nodding wake inspires a rattled breath,
But sounds distinct are rare and growing thin.
Distractions serve distraction's last request:
To tinker, tapping time on hammered tin.

If buried losses rise to days unspent,
Write the priest and draw upon the rent.

I

That diary she kept sometime
Of a princess castled in New York
Has arrived as planned to give
The Midnight Cowboys a view.

Through the oily windshields
And primary glare of red, green, blue,
Note the mirrors, the asphalt
And the varnishing rain.

Fabricate the smooth finish,
Between the juicy pores
On the beloved skin
Of our teenage whore.

With no lawn to keep in suburbia,
Equivocal, unsure, the issue
Manufactures in hidden plants
A reel possessed by strangers.

II

It's the daily blow by blow,
Left, right broad casted show
Of Rocky Marciano not losing
His cherry to Jersey Joe.

Why struggle to uncork
The celebratory fizz of some
Stake-in-the-heart victory
Over Jones next door?

As she said, we are all betrayed
By the obsessive love that excludes
All the chorus and wants all
From others once adored.

Semper Fi

Light rain greased the streets
Under orange street lights.
I prod along up hill
Trying to squeeze
The outside in, the inside out.
Beside me in the gutter
A jaunty boat sails down stream
As morning light
Makes the vapor blink away.

I awoke with a sad start
After another final no.
Things will never be done again
And will not come back.
I know I in the dream
Are nailing down finality
And will rehearse it until the night
Is lost in the rushing
Stream of mourning.

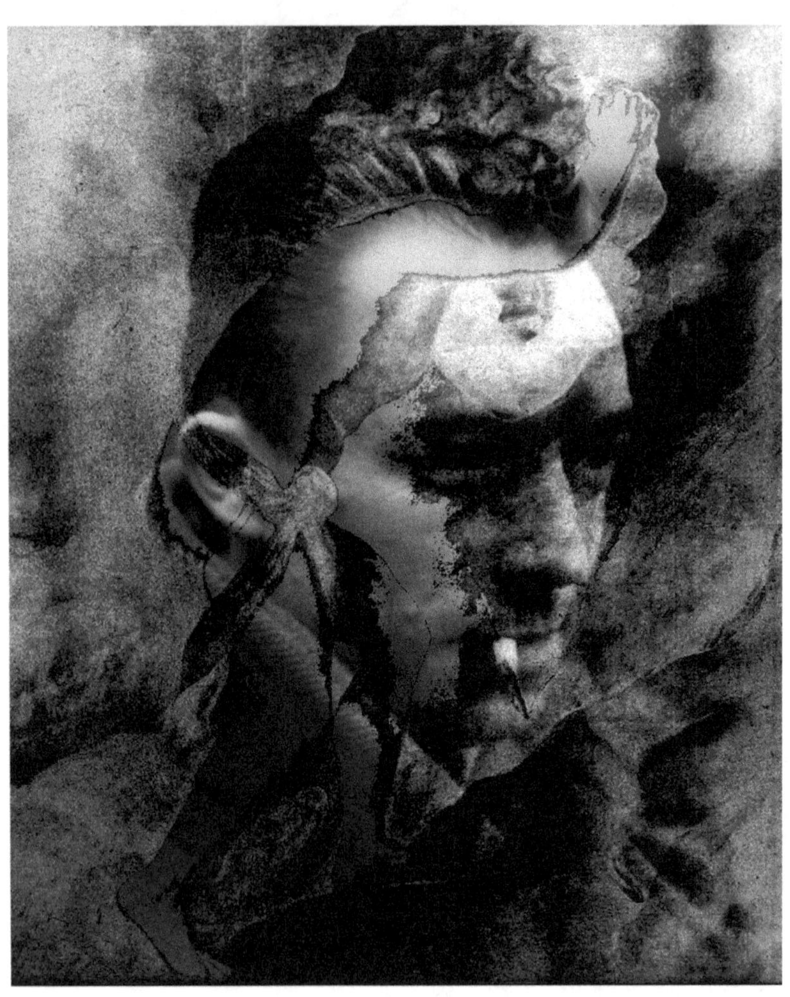

When rolling up a hill the final time
A rock less heavy than the night before,
We reckon nymphs have turned away inclined
To cast their sweetest eye to jobs less boring.

For them, sun and day are drawing moisture
To fill the glades with dew refreshing night.
Our cliff's a distant wrinkle, our grunts the voice
Of granules trickling down the narrowed pipe.

The sounds that fill the lines and addled themes,
Of elder gentlemen whose rock is raised
Above the gravel sliding pass the dream,
Are pairs of words to slip in waiting places.

For timeless beauties betting martingale
Encumbered rhyme inscribes the cycles failing.

I

For devils gouging zinc and leaving burrs
On rollers, beds and tools for making prints,
A deeper anger cuts the face unfurled,
Insulted, blotted, nicked by stranger dents.

Corroded plots, sunk in acid baths,
Exposed among the stories others left,
Resisting time the sticky ground's a mask
As soured currents lift the etching's theft.

Conspire, anneal the metal, harden wood
In fire to save the meek and helpless core.
Burins raising light to darken mood,
Smooth the dimpled grain of shades explored.

First impressions struck from copper plate,
Are written thick and thin to burnish proof,
While scales of mezzo tints will moderate
The fertile work repeating crowded truth.

II

The gravers irony awoke a crafty demon.
Manufacture signs a person but keeps
The habits still repeating scripts as freedom.
Pamphlets swerve rebellions, strangers meet.

The gravid press is kin to bedded pairs.
Its sheets and blankets duplicate the urge
To mate and roll again the self in heirs,
To dominate, to duplicate the scourge.

As cities trade the gleaming gods for coin
And heads of state engrave the value given,
Are these machines to pry apart the loins
And pull the birthing tract still hidden?

In long editions each impression fades,
The first are rare, the last softly wiped
To kindly end what once was clearly made:
A breeding printer inking sharpened type.

I

Were I to tease the world apart and pinch
The spinning tale of each atom at hand
So it emits an amusing squeal of light,
Or if, by arming phantasms with mining picks,
I would unseal the chest, uncork the urn,
And so end the sense of dying out of worlds,
Would I, a Buddha, know the self is blindness?

Our true picture is not a phenotype,
Displaying elements applied as rules to living,
A show and tell that's but a trace in clouds
Of codes and meanings and lines drawn to stop
Unsheltered above a canvas wanting paint.
Or is it? Brush away the dust revealing
Cracks, the steps in each eternal moment.

Why would humans, armed with
knowledge of what is
themselves necessarily
To merely persist?
persisting is, or can be,
pleasant?
Someday the ideas of self-
and competitive struggle will be
metaphysics or horror stories
— mold armor @ home depot —
1 gal of water, cup bleach
1 gal of plain water

II

The child never sleeps to dream of dreams
Unreal, and seldom grows beyond the trade
Of love for kindness, gaining loving friend.
With tin cups and empty tuna cans
And rising banners, crepes of orange and blue,
The shrine of mental flesh entombs the bargain,
The missing action becomes majestic sadness.

Idol worship adds a dab of gold,
Reflects the ambient light of shade as sun.
It colors drab ledgers of skills acquired,
Gives economy to idle time,
Demonstrates the fetal demons prolifers ate,
Employs no longer lines of working dead
And funny caps our call for Godly anger.

BEWEGUNG

The blanket begged the cooling night to stay,
To prove the wheezing rights of men infirm,
To squeeze the wool and dream the clock away,
To tuck their innards back beneath concern.

When elders stoop to dibble daisy seed,
Or nibble interest paid by hidden hands,
Will care decry the trade of song for weed
As suns are counted more than mother lands.

If fruit has sides unseen by leaves on high
And each receives the weight to ripen earth,
With seeds and snakes and rhizomes sneaking by,
Then whithered man will wail alone his birth.

You old and soiled and rotten garden boots,
You kicked the cane to kill the creeping root.

I

Thirteen straight razors that draw
Bristles on a tender face,
Would prosecute us for philandering
And sell indulgences to advance
The writ issued on propagation.

Stiffly determined by hormonal doses
Promoting usefulness and dire necessity,
The continuing feast on gluttons,
Lets puritans squeak a living
From plagues, impurities and predestination.

Turkeys trots by black holes
Halt expanding vapors passed above
To abate or disaprovingly approve,
To debate or raise ruckus,
In hells of congressional resentment.

The hollow hall of rectitude,
May children blow them down,
Like our daily financial bubbles,
Invented by fast and furious
Celebrants of tradition's last party.

Axions are true despite solitude.
They dispel the sulfurous gas
Of floating speech in Cartoon.
Wracking whites cheroot the plantation
And bombast the multicultural pollutions.

II

The smoke emitted naming nothing,
No one here One Eye
But the cold dark matter
Trading wine on transparent seas
In dreams of early poets.

Pirates, capitalized by teenage queens,
Sack the gold and slaves
Of rival corporations sailing westerlies.
They are the prophets edge
Slicing through the jungle's hedge.

On the steppes the advantage
Of long grass feeding stallions
And harem mares or colts
Is flattened by rolling armies
The dressage of chicken colonels.

Quadrupedic memory in reviewing stands
Rebukes the dodger's nimble hand,
Sighs when equestrian statues fail
To roundup patrons trotting pass
Histories of pocket picking flattery.

III

In judgment the will decides
To give half the child
To each side, but then
Turns upon the simple trick
To suckle truth with sentiment.

Literature and guilty leisure live
Side by side in cities
Where savants set the level,
Servants the cord descending bob,
That plumbs the windowed eye.

Parallel such allegory will remind
The workers of patchwork manikins,
Dictators of fashion that's One
More monolith composed of reasons
To shake the invisible hand.

To keep the asshole high
You remold devil dung Diogenes
To represent the slaughtered lamb.
Take deep breath and hold
An opening for useless revelry.

Do they believe midwives skilled in craft
When working, feel that friction drives,
That some resistance helps move the task,
And guides the screaming push of labor's bride?

Intercourse with solid things evokes a song
Or sigh, the flowing rhythm conducts the grace.
Nature though has eyes and tongues for longing
And halts the blade that branching knots embrace.

Do they imagine enduring Atlas received his pay?
The strain of holding spheres aloft didn't kill.
Those new to measured tasks and elder ways
Can't sign the mythic note for reason's bill.

That hard is better makes fools of man.
The lordling's sky is mother's rosy hand.

The trumpet cannot bite,
Though a review may imagine it.
But here it comes,
Prodded from behind
By the lax soldier,
Cynically employed,
But paid with brotherhood.

Vis a Tergo is wind funneled
Through the brazen tubes
To herald a metaphysics
And part the sheep from peasants.
The enclosures, ha-ha, trip
Simpletons for the pleasure
Of garden views expansive.

Should we too late
Protest the perilous heading
The younger take?

Off the map
We play a fiddle
On the generation gap.

Sitting like a bear
Who once dancing
Now just stares.

The blank space
Is still opening
At a slower pace.

But so what?
All the blare and honking
Kept the windows shut.

The compass only proves
Poles are switching
Lodestones are being moved.

The speck your eye has caught
Was fleeting charm.
A quirk confounded twice
By blunt desire
And tears for clearing
The foreign thing,
Myopic debris
That is itself
A warning
Of harm
Congealed
In godly
Fear.

www.ingramcontent.com/pod-product-compliance
Lightning Source LLC
LaVergne TN
LVHW050643100826
845148LV00011B/1956